Concession Stand Fundraising

RICK AND BECKY KRAEMER

CONTENTS

RICK AND BECKY KRAEMER

1 INTRODUCTION

Non-profit organizations have a variety of fundraising opportunities available to them. They range from direct request campaigns, ("Please give us money!"), to selling products or services. Many of these options waste valuable volunteer time. For example, consider the classic car wash fundraiser. You gather 20 volunteers on a Saturday morning with soap and cardboard signs, charging passers-by $5 to wash their cars. Four hours later, you've raised $300. It seems successful until you do the math and realize your volunteers have each earned $3.75 per hour. That's not a bad effort if your volunteers are school children, but if adult volunteers are taking time off from work or other important activities to wash cars at slave wages, you're wasting their time. The chief advantage of a well-run concession stand is that adult volunteers can earn upward of $20 per hour for your organization, without having to get wet and soapy, or sunburned.

2 ARE CONCESSIONS THE RIGHT FUNDRAISER FOR YOU?

While concessions are an excellent fundraising choice, they may not be a good fit with your organization. Before committing to concessions, consider the following successful stand traits:

Will you have a hungry and thirsty crowd? First and foremost, will your stand have a hungry crowd of people close by, or even better, walking past? You won't sell much to a small group that has just eaten. But if you have a captive group attending a hot outdoor concert, it's a perfect opportunity to sell cold beverages, snacks and ice cream treats. Or you can sell warm beverages and hot dogs during a cold football game. The key is to have a crowd that's both hungry and motivated to purchase your products.

Will there be any competition? Concession Stands are most successful in isolated spots where customers don't have any other choices, and would have to drive to the nearest alternative. The best locations are sports fields, events on school campuses, rural events, and other events where it's inconvenient to leave the building or fenced area. Once we volunteered at a stand in the middle of a large, remote park filled with baseball diamonds and soccer fields. The city had provided a wonderful, permanent facility, but they had also allowed several soda vending machines to be placed just a few feet from the building's concession counter. We were forced to charge less than the vending machine prices because any time there was a line at our stand, people began buying from the vending machines instead of our stand.

You should also avoid opening your stand near commercial vendors like restaurants, grocery stores, or a deli. They will compete with you for sales and you won't be able to raise as much money. You'll also be eroding their business, creating animosity with the local merchant, damaging your non-profit organization's relationship with the community.

Can you open the concession stand often enough? It takes time to "dial in" your concession stand, so you'll want to open it more than once. You may be able to operate a yearly concession stand successfully, but it will take a couple of years to figure out how much will sell, and avoid either under or over stocking (more on this later). Because unused food will eventually spoil, it is much better to run your concession stand monthly, weekly or even more frequently than it is to start it up and shut it down after months of inactivity. Most snack foods have a long shelf life, but if it will be more than 3 months between openings, you will have to close out your inventory each time you close down.

Do you have a large enough pool of responsible, reliable volunteers? Do you remember your grade school lemonade stand? All of your friends wanted to be your partner instead of your customers, and spent most of their time coercing you into free samples – if your parents hadn't provided the materials for free, you wouldn't have made a dime. You can employ some underage volunteers, but there will be abundant cash, sanitary requirements, and other responsibilities that require adult supervision. You'll need a pool of willing adults large enough to cover all of the shifts. Shifts should have at least 2 volunteers, and shouldn't exceed 4 hours (less if it is hot).

Are snack foods available for a bulk discount? Profit is the difference between the cost you pay for an item and what you sell it for. It's the amount of money you "make," so you want low costs and high prices. You can't pay grocery store prices for your products and still make a good profit; you'll need a way to get items in bulk at low wholesale prices. Warehouse stores and clubs are prevalent, so you can get candy and sodas in bulk packs of 30 or more at near wholesale prices. If you don't have one of these locally, you may be able to set up an arrangement with a local store to purchase products at their cost; you might as well ask them to donate the products, just in case they are willing, but don't return to them so often that you become a nuisance.

Is a facility available? You'll need to buy, borrow, rent or build a booth, bar, tables or cart to sell your products from. Will your faculty have countertops, electricity, refrigeration, storage, and security? Is someone able to build a stand or cart for you (at what cost?), or will you purchase folding tables and a collapsible canopy? Will your volunteers and products need protection from the elements? Your facility may limit the products you are able to offer.

Will you have adequate storage? You need to store your products between openings. Does your concession stand have adequate storage faculties, or can you easily transport your products back and forth to a secure storage facility? The products will need protection from pilferage, pests like bugs and animals, and the elements. Chocolate will melt in the heat, and canned beverages will explode when frozen. Make sure you consider these issues before storing your products in someone's garage.

<u>Are there laws and regulations that apply?</u> Most states with sales tax will exempt the sale of prepackaged food for fundraising, but you should check your state's rules on foods that you heat or otherwise prepare at http://www.fundraisetaxlaw.org. Local rules for permitting, advertising, and sanitation vary widely, so check with your state, county, and city on any special rules that apply. We read recently about a group that was cited for giving away free water and coffee at Mardi Gras without a permit and sales license! Alcohol sales are very profitable, but you have to comply with additional rules and regulations, which vary by locale.

<u>Are the start-up and overhead costs reasonable?</u> How much money will you need to spend before you can open the first day? You may need to spend initial money on facilities, cooking appliances and utensils, and storage containers before you even buy your food products. How long will you have to operate to cover these initial costs? How much change will you need in the cash box each day before you open? What recurring costs (also called overhead) will you pay in addition to the cost of your products? Is there a yearly fee or rental charge for the facility, a cost for electricity, or for ice? Will some of your products require disposable items like cups, plates, utensils, bags, napkins, or condiments? Will you need trash can liners and cleaning supplies? See the worksheet in the appendices to help you organize and total these costs.

If you can answer "Yes" to all of these questions, you are ready to start planning your concession stand. If your answer is a qualified "Yes", or "No" to some of them, don't give up yet. With a little creativity, you may still be able to get around some of your obstacles.

3 FACILITIES

Once you've decided that concessions fit your fundraising requirements and organization, you'll need to secure a facility. Your concession stand can be as simple as hawker trays (like the vendors carry up and down the stands in professional baseball games), or as sophisticated as a permanent building with a commercial kitchen. At the most basic level, you'll need a place to display products and a place to collect money; you can start with as little as a folding table and an envelope of $1 bills. Starting up is easier in an existing facility, but they may limit what products you can sell; conversely, if you have specific products you want to sell, like popcorn, they will dictate your facility's features, like electricity.

The first facility consideration is shelter from the elements. If you're outdoors, you'll need to protect volunteers and products from inclement weather. You don't want your chocolate bars and volunteers melting in the sun, or getting soggy in the rain, so you'll need a roof. You can purchase or borrow a collapsible canopy, portable shed, wheeled cart or concession trailer. As a non-profit, your best option is to have volunteers or another organization buy, build or donate a facility to you. As you consider your options, also include security for your volunteers, products, and cash.

The next facility consideration is utilities. Coolers can help you sell without refrigeration, but if you're preparing food, it is very convenient to have running water, allowing volunteers to wash their hands and wash dishes. You can always throw your dirty dishes into a tub to wash later, but it is easier on volunteers if there is a sink available for dish washing (we'll spend more time late discussing volunteer burnout). If you're planning to operate after dark or serve hot foods (which create higher profits), you're also going to need electricity. Electricity allows you to light a dark area, heat a cold space, warm or cook foods, and refrigerate beverages. Many outdoor facilities have a place to plug in an extension cord, but you may need keys to access the receptacle. Be safe with electricity; when running extension cords outdoors, make sure you are plugged into a Ground Fault Circuit Interrupter (GFCI) to prevent accidental electrocution.

Storage is also a big consideration when acquiring a facility. You will need to store your cooking appliances and utensils, as well as protecting your products from theft, insects, vermin, and extreme temperatures. If your facility is outdoors and primitive, you may need to haul all of your supplies and equipment in and out each day you are open, and then store them in someone's house (remember that food in garages attracts undesirable little creatures). Ideally, you'll be in a securely locked facility with heat and air conditioning, with plenty of bug- and rodent-proof cabinets to store equipment and excess stock.

Finally, consider garbage and janitorial. Most of your products will generate trash from wrappers and packaging, so you'll need receptacles where your customers can throw away their trash and uneaten food. In states where there are deposits on beverage containers, you may also want to provide recycle bins. You'll want to clarify who is responsible for providing trash can liners and emptying the trash cans. You'll also want to check on the cost of rent, if any, and whether it includes janitorial services (and janitorial charges).

4 PRODUCT SELECTION

Once you've secured your facility, your next step will be deciding what products to sell, but your facility may place limits on the products you can sell. For example, if your facility doesn't have electricity you probably won't sell frozen ice cream, but you could haul in iced beverages. Chocolate bars melt in the sun, but sugared candy is very durable and preserves well. Canned beverages are impervious to pests, but are heavy to haul long distances, and prone to explode when frozen. Electricity is convenient for heating or cooking food, as is water for appliance and utensil cleaning. In addition to facility limitations, here are some other factors to consider when you're deciding what to sell:

What can I sell for a profit? What can you purchase at a bulk discount? A research trip to the local warehouse market's candy and beverage aisles is a good place to start your research. We'll talk more about pricing later, but you can use vending machine prices as an initial price target for your research. **You should try to make about 100% profit**, so you need to purchase your products for half of what you sell them for. That means if candy bars and sodas are selling for $1 in local vending machines, you'll need to get them in bulk for about $0.50 each. If you're taking over an existing concession stand, don't assume that every product you're currently selling is making you money – do your homework and confirm that all of your products are profitable. When you're calculating your profit, you also need to include any extra costs you'll incur with that product. Does your state charge a deposit on beverage containers (don't assume everyone will return them to your recycle bins)? Will you need to provide disposable containers like cups, plates, boxes or bags? Will you provide utensils, napkins, or condiments? Does the product require disposable gloves for handling, or special cooking and cleaning supplies? If you serve coffee, you'll need cups, cream, sugar, and stir sticks. All of these will increase your

7

product's cost, so make sure you calculate them in. If you need help with this calculation, see the chapter on math for guidance.

How much variety do I need? Since your customers will have different tastes, you'll want a reasonable selection of products. For example, if you are selling sodas, you'll want provide at least a cola, a diet drink, and a non-cola, which covers most soda tastes. If you are selling a high volume, you can also consider slower selling specialty sodas like root beer or other flavors. **As much as possible, you should give customers choices between salty, sugary, and high fat products.** Popcorn, potato chips and salted nuts are popular in the salty category, candies cater to the sugary & sweet tastes, and pastries, chocolate bars and most meats cover the high fat choices. One thing to be aware of is the economic principle of substitution. This says that **if your customers can't get exactly what they want, they will often choose something similar.** For example, if your customers can't get chocolate with nuts in it, they will probably choose either chocolate with a crunchy filling or an item with nuts. The principle of substitution says that you don't need every possible brand of snack item; you just need a reasonable representative of each kind of snack, beverage, or hot food, so your customers can pick an alternative to what they really wanted.

What special appliances will be required? Many popular concession products are prepared on specialized appliances, which can be expensive and difficult for your volunteers to learn how to use. Snow cones and cotton candy are very profitable, but require special, commercial machines. Scooped ice cream requires freezers that open from the top, unless you sell pre-packaged treats like popsicles and ice cream bars and sandwiches. Commercial hotdog rollers are convenient, but electric skillets are an inexpensive substitute. Commercial popcorn poppers start at around $400 for counter-top models. However, some items that usually require special equipment can just be heated in a microwave, like microwave popcorn, corn dogs, and soft pretzels. For the other items, **do you have access to the special appliances required, or are you able to purchase them?**

How much preparation and clean up time is needed for the product? Do you have to make a separate shopping trip to get one special item? How early do volunteers need to show up to start cooking or heating hot items? Speaking of volunteers, you'll be really tempted to have volunteers prepare homemade items; everyone donates the materials, so it seems like you won't incur any costs. We strongly recommend that you **stay away from bake sales** – between baking and delivery they aren't an efficient use of your volunteer's time (more on volunteer burnout later), the products don't preserve well until the next time you open, and it is difficult to get a consistent product inventory over the long term. Also consider how late the volunteers need to stay cleaning up after each of the products. Many coffee shops now provide pre-made coffee in large reusable or disposable containers, which are a great alternate to scheduling volunteers early so they can start the percolator. Pre-packaged foods like candy, chocolate bars, fruit snacks, breakfast bars, canned and bottled beverages, and chips are all good choices, because they don't require special sanitation handling, extra preparation, or cleanup.

What will be popular? Make sure to consider the weather and local preferences. If it's going to be hot out, stock plenty of ice cold water **(always have bottled water – it will be your highest profit item)** and other canned and bottled cold beverages, and think about selling ice cream bars or making blended ice drinks like iced coffee or fruit smoothies. Chocolate candy bars don't sell well in the heat, because they are messy and don't cool you down, but if you have a freezer chocolate coated ice cream and popsicles will fly out of your stand. If it is going to be cold, stock coffee, tea, hot chocolate and hot cider, as well as hot foods. Remember that many people now stop by the coffee shop first before driving to an event, so don't go crazy on the coffee the first time. Athletes will prefer sport drinks, and young people will purchase energy drinks over sodas.

Local preferences will also determine what will sell. Some regions expect nachos at their concession stands, while others expect Sloppy Joes, barbeque, or other local favorites. Hot Dogs and popcorn are universal favorites. If the crowd will be mostly adults in a contained area, consider serving alcohol (check local regulations carefully; in California volunteer bartenders can't take cash, so you need a separate station to sell "drink tickets"). If the customers will be more health conscious, stock up on real fruit juice, nuts, trail mix, granola bars and other healthy packaged foods, and consider selling organic fruit (start fruit slowly – it doesn't preserve well).

In the end, the products you sell will be limited by your facility's features, and what you can buy at bulk discounts. You'll choose based on products that can make a substantial profit, are appropriate for the weather, and are popular with local tastes. Finally, you must limit yourself to products that are reasonable to transport, store, prepare, and clean up after.

5 PRICING

After you've researched potential products to sell, you'll need to decide how much to charge for your items. If you don't have any idea where to start, begin with the prices being charged in local vending machines. If sodas and candy bars are selling for $1.25, and you can buy them in bulk for less than $0.60, you can charge $1 for sodas. When pricing water, candy bars, and other products that come in different sizes, make sure you are comparing prices with similar sizes, or price per ounce. We'll talk later about how to do this math in case you need a refresher course. You can also research other concession stands and their pricing, but don't use professional sports arenas to set your prices, because they can get away with charging much more than you can.

In your pricing, you need markups that will make you money, but are not so high that people won't buy from you. People expect to pay much more at a concession stand than they do at their grocery store, but they have their limits. In general, you should be able to mark everything up at least 50% (take half of the cost, and add it to the full cost, so a $1 item sells for $1.50), **but you should set your goal at 100% markup (you sell the product for double what you paid for it, so a $1 item sells for $2).** Make sure to add extra costs (containers, deposits, condiments) in your cost before your markup price. For example, if sodas cost you $0.65, and have a $0.05 deposit, your actual cost is $0.70, so you'd like to sell it for double of your actual cost, or $1.40. Check out the math chapter for how to make these calculations, as well as splitting other costs like cups and utensils across the cost of an item. **If you can't get at least a 50% markup, you shouldn't sell the item.**

There are a few products with outlandish profit margins; go ahead and use high mark-ups if your items will sell for high prices. Water is the best example of this – you buy it for pennies, and sell it for $1 or $2 depending on the size of the bottle. Even if you have to pay a deposit, the markup is typically hundreds of percent, so **bottled water is one of your most profitable products;** we'll talk more about this when we talk about stocking, but you always want to have extra water, since it is cheap, stores well, and is highly profitable. You should make a high profit on foods that you prepare in the stand, since your labor is "free" from the volunteers. Hot dogs, popcorn, hot chocolate and other foods that you heat or cook should be marked up at least 200% (the cost times 4).

It's tempting to pick prices that give you the maximum profit for each item, like charging $1.25 for a candy bar that costs you $0.50, because that is the market price in local vending machines. However, you also want to factor buyer psychology into your pricing. **Your real goal not to make the most profit on each item, it is to empty your customer's wallet on each sale (it's for a good cause, right?).** For example, a parent might give their child $2 and send them to your concession stand. If all of your items are priced at $1.25, you will only sell $1.25 worth of product, and the child will take $0.75 back to their parent. However, if your items are all $1, you'll sell $2 worth of product. In the first case, you've profited $0.75, but in the second case you've made $1. Another example of poor psychological pricing is buying a large tub of licorice, and re-packaging it in baggies for $0.25 each. When a child purchases the licorice with their dollar, you lose $0.75 in income. Finally, with the wide use of charge cards, people aren't used to carrying coins, so they prefer to get even dollar amounts back instead of coins. If an item just doesn't make sense at an even dollar amount, you can **use specials to entice customers into using up the rest of their change on another purchase**. For example, if a can of soda really should be $1.50, but won't sell well at $2, mark sodas at $2 and throw in a free bag of popcorn with each soda, or have a special "value meal" where a soda and a hot dog are $3.

6 STOCKING – HOW MUCH TO PURCHASE

Once you've completed your product research, and determined your prices, you have to decide how many items to purchase for resale. This is called "stocking" or purchasing "stock inventory." **If you don't have enough of a product at your concession stand, you'll sell out everything early**, won't have anything left to sell, and will miss out on money you could have made. We talked with one organization that purchased a semi-truck trailer of refrigerated water for an activity on the asphalt tarmac of an airport. That's an awful lot of bottled water. The event was scheduled to run for 3 hours, but it was a very hot day, and there weren't any drinking fountains, so they sold out an entire semi-truck trailer of cold water in 30 minutes! Conversely, **if you purchase too much of a product, you won't be able to sell all of it and may experience cash flow issues** (all of your money is in product inventory, so you can't pay for anything else), or the extra stock may spoil before you open again.

If you're just not sure at all where to start, then assume 20% of the crowd will buy a beverage (size of the crowd times 0.2), 10% will purchase a packaged snack item (size of the crowd times 0.1) and 5% of the crowd will purchase a cooked or heated item (crowd size times 0.05). You can start with these numbers, and either try to adjust them based on your situations, or purchase more than you need the first day. As you consider how to adjust your sales estimates, think through the following situations that may impact your purchasing:

<u>What are my transportation restrictions?</u> How are you going to transport the products you purchase, and will the vehicle have enough room and weight capacity for everything? If the volunteer who purchases and transports the products drives a subcompact car, they won't be able to haul around many beverage cases, due to both space and weight carrying limitations. If they drive a pickup truck, will they be leaving the products

unsecured in the bed of the truck, where they are susceptible to theft, heat, or cold? Do frozen products like ice cream bars require extra cooling during transportation?

How far away is the store from the concession stand? Is it convenient to run back to the store each day the stand is open, or even in the middle of a shift, if you run out of an item? If you're just starting out, and the store isn't too far away, you can start with less than you think you'll need, and run to the store for more in the middle or at the end of the day. Remember that you don't want to burn out your volunteers by stressing them with panicked runs to the store for extra hot dogs and buns, so you'll want to arrange this responsibility with a volunteer who isn't serving at the concession stand.

What kind of storage is available? The size, type, and location of your storage will limit how much product you can purchase, especially items that need refrigeration or freezing. Feel free to stock up on items that can be stored on-site at the stand, but limit stock on items that require special transportation and storage. For example, if storage in your stand is secure from theft and pests, but not heat, you can store extra beverages and canned foods, but not chocolate bars.

If you don't have storage space at the concession stand, or it is inadequate, you'll have to haul all of your products back and forth. If you can avoid it, you don't want to haul extra products into and out of the stand each day. If your stand isn't open consecutive days, then you may not be able to store the extra stock in a vehicle, requiring the extra step of loading from your storage site into the vehicle, and then unloading the vehicle into the stand. In the same way, after you load the vehicle at the end of the day, you'll need to unload the vehicle once again into off-site storage. That doubles the number of times that someone has to lift and carry those heavy beverage cases. Canned and bottled items can often stay in the stand, but without refrigeration you'll need to take hot dogs and ice cream out each night.

What preserves well? If you purchase a large quantity of a product, will it expire before you can sell it? **We recommend that you always buy more bottled water than you can possibly sell.** It should be one of your most profitable products, is very inexpensive to stock, and lasts for a very long time. Bottled water is such a great opportunity to make money, with no disadvantage to having extra (unless you have to move it around), so you always want to end the day with an extra case or two of bottled water. On the other hand, meats and breads will spoil quickly, so you'll want to manage their stock levels carefully, or be forced to throw away food that won't keep until the next time the stand opens.

What is the size of your cash and crowd? Depending on your organization's finances, your initial stocking may be limited by the amount of cash available. If your non-profit has plenty of cash to "front" you, you can purchase as much stock as you'd like, and pay back the advance from the concession profits. However, many non-profits run on very little cash, so you may be limited by the ability of your volunteer shopper to "Float" the cash needed for the initial purchases. They may also need to make the purchases on a credit card, so you'll need to generate enough profits to reimburse them within 25 days. If you are limited by cash, you'll want to start with just a handful of products, until you can observe typical buying habits. Once you know how much of the core or basic products to purchase each time, you can start to experiment with more unusual products. With the exception of bottled water, **start with less than you think you'll need; if you sell out of one or more items, you can always get more next time**. If you buy too much, it can take a very long time to get rid of it, and you may even be forced to give it away at the end of the season instead of allowing it to spoil. With water, you'll always want to buy more than you think you'll need, because it is cheap to purchase, highly profitable, and can easily be stored until the next time you're open.

It's easiest to estimate your stocking needs from records of previous sales, but if you're starting from scratch, then assume 20% of the crowd will buy a beverage (size of the crowd times 0.2), 10% will purchase a packaged snack item (size of the crowd times 0.1) and 5% of the crowd will purchase a cooked or heated item (crowd times 0.05). These numbers will be smaller than what you can usually sell, but are a good place to start if you just don't have a clue how much stock to buy for the first time, and aren't impacted by any of the restrictions mentioned above.

7 VOLUNTEERS

Unless you have a small, fleeting concession stand, you're going to need copious volunteers selling, purchasing, training, advertising, delivering, banking, accounting and even more. You'll face three difficult challenges coordinating volunteers. **They are 1) recruiting volunteers, 2) getting them assigned and committed to work, and 3) preventing burnout so they'll keep volunteering.**

First, you'll recruit volunteers who operate the different parts of the concession stand. **Most people take up a volunteer position because they are personally asked to "join up."** You can post advertisements for your needs (include a short job description of each volunteer opportunity), or make announcement at large gatherings, but you'll get most of your volunteers by asking them yourself in a conversation. The best volunteer recruiters are people with great relationship building and personal interaction skills – social people who network well. If you have a large enough organization you can appoint a "volunteer coordinator" or even a committee to recruit and schedule all of your volunteers. It also helps if the existing volunteers are happy and having fun, because happy volunteers attract more volunteers (see the section on preventing volunteer burnout); who wouldn't want to hang out with happy, fun people? We also find that volunteers are more willing to commit if the opportunity has an end date. It is easier to get volunteers if they don't feel like they're making an irrevocable, lifelong commitment to concessions. We recommend that you invite volunteers to a one-time "trial" activity where they test the waters, and then ask them to commit to volunteering for a specific time frame, like a sport's season or a certain number of concession stand openings.

Second, you need to *schedule* volunteers to coordinate, purchase, train, deliver, set up, staff the stand, and clean up afterward. Many volunteer coordinators and directors complain that scheduling volunteers is their least favorite task, causing them to eventually give up a volunteer leadership role that they otherwise enjoy. Much of this pain comes from chasing down individuals and coercing them into "volunteering" for open slots on the schedule. Once we get our list of "willing" volunteers (some organizations require a minimum number of volunteers hours, so volunteers are not exactly excited about their volunteer opportunities), **we've always felt the perfect freedom to assign people to time slots.** We try to poll them first to find out where they are interested ("Do you have specific dates you would like to work, or prior commitments where you can't work?"), and accommodate where possible, but we generally don't get much feedback, and just tell people when they are expected to show up. Surprisingly, we get very few requests to swap shifts when we do this. There are many internet tools available to help with this process, from email to shared documents like Google's, to volunteer web sites that email volunteer reminders a few days in advance. The size of your volunteer pool should determine how sophisticated your electronic volunteer tracking system needs to be. **For us, the key is to tell people when they are scheduled, and let them work out any conflicts on their own with the rest of the team.**

Finally, you'll need to keep your volunteers from burning out. If you deal with volunteers often, we strongly recommend reading Bill Hybels' book *The Volunteer Revolution: Unleashing the Power of Everybody*. It is focused on volunteerism in churches, but has an excellent premise that if you figure out what volunteers like to do, and encourage them occasionally, they will be happy volunteering for years without burning out. In the context of concession stands, you may be stuck with a few volunteers who really don't enjoy what they're doing, but have to contribute to the organization, so keeping them from burning out is even more important.

So, how do you prevent volunteer burnout? **Volunteers burn out and quit because they are either tired, frustrated, or both.** The easiest way to counteract volunteer exhaustion and frustration is to recognize their contributions. Volunteer recognition can be as simple as a handwritten thank-you note, or as complex as an encouragement system with gifts, awards and prizes. At minimum, volunteers should be verbally and sincerely thanked for their help at every possible occasion. The important thing is to make sure volunteers feel appreciated for the sacrifices they are making; these small recognitions prevent burn-out and motivate volunteers to keep working hard. Companionship also keeps volunteers from burning out. **Few people want to work totally alone; it is much more fun to do volunteer activities with other people or with a team**, if only so they have someone else to complain with. Plus, we find that most people interested in staffing shifts at the concession stand are outgoing and social, so they need someone to interact with. For these reasons, we try to always have people work together as teams of two or more whenever they volunteer.

There are many situations that wear out and exasperate volunteers. When they are asked to do something they didn't expect, they quickly become tired and frustrated. This happens when volunteers are signed up for a single shift, but then have to do a second shift because the next volunteer doesn't show up for their shift. Another exasperating situation arises when volunteers are forced into making a "diving save" like taking unplanned shopping trips to re-stock the stand. You'll also violate their expectations when you ask them to do a job they haven't signed up for, either because the concession roles are unclear, or the responsibilities are disorganized and uncertain. If you're splitting responsibilities and roles among a large group of volunteers, it's worth taking the time to write some one-paragraph job descriptions to be clear about what is being asked of volunteers. They'll get frustrated if they perceive that other volunteers aren't pulling their fair share of work or hours. Also beware the martyr who volunteers for everything because they think they have to, then resents that they're doing all the work. **Volunteers will burn out if they don't have the resources they need to be successful, like clearly posted prices, supplies, and adequate change in the cash drawer.** They also need both guidelines to give them direction (it is best if these are written and posted), and enough autonomy to make decisions if something unusual comes up. For example, be careful that you don't have a control freak with a strong personality demanding thinks be done their way and ordering people around. Your volunteers are adults – if you ask them to do things a specific way, explain why it is important (e.g. disposable gloves are required to meet sanitation regulations), which **shows your respect for their intelligence, and equips them to make good choices when something unexpected occurs.**

8 EQUIPMENT, SUPPLIES, SETUP AND CLEANUP

The equipment you'll need, supplies you'll provide, and setup required will vary widely. They depend on facility features, or more importantly what isn't available in your facility, as well as the products you've chosen to sell. We've included a list of possible equipment and supplies you may need in the appendices, so check there to make sure you haven't forgotten anything.

There are some preparation tasks that you can do hours or even days before you open the concession stand. Here are pre-work ideas you can add to your checklist:

✓ Get change from the bank for the cash drawer
✓ Shop for products and supplies
✓ Pick up keys, arrange to have the facility unlocked, or pack up tables and awning
✓ Collect cooking equipment and utensils
✓ Collect other supplies (clear plastic tubs work well for supplies)

At the concession stand, you'll have a number of pre-opening tasks. Here is a list of ideas to add to your checklist:

✓ Unpack and transport supplies and equipment
✓ Set up tables and awnings if needed
✓ Connect electricity and water if needed
✓ Begin heating hot items and icing or refrigerating cold items
✓ Post prices for your products
✓ Set out a sample of each product so customers can see what you are selling

After you're done for the day, you'll need to clean up. We recommend that you pre-package the last of your hot food, and clean the cooking appliances while you continue to sell. You may also need to do some or all of the following:

- ✓ Wash equipment and utensils
- ✓ Count and record the money in the cash drawer
- ✓ Do an inventory by counting how much is left (may not be needed every time)
- ✓ Pack up products, supplies and equipment
- ✓ Lock the facility
- ✓ Transport supplies and equipment
- ✓ Deliver the cash

These are just a few of the tasks you may want to put in a checklist for your volunteers. The facility you use and the products you sell will determine what you'll add or remove from these lists.

9 MARKETING AND ADVERTISING

The best marketing you can provide is a conspicuous location with aromatic food. When people see and smell your food, they will be impulsively attracted to your concession stand. After you've assured the sight and smell of your stand, you may also consider running some of the additional marketing and advertising campaigns proposed in this chapter.

If your stand is supporting a major event, let people know that concessions will be available during the event. Notify customers that they can come to the event hungry, with money in hand, and you'll take care of them. If possible, you'd like to do this by **co-advertising with the event**. Co-advertising means that if the event is marketing with posters, radio and television announcements, email or social networking, they would also add your advertising. When you are working with event planners, ask them to include a small note or advertisement to posters and announcements like, "Concessions provided by …" or "Mention this add to get a special deal at the concession stand." During the event, ask the MC or announcer to make periodic announcements advertising both your concession stand and your non-profit organization – people are willing to spend money on expensive concessions if they know the profits are going to a good cause, and you may even recruit new members. Run hourly specials, giving the MC a list of your specials and when to announce them. If sales are slow, have someone walk around with one of your visually recognizable and strong smelling products, like popcorn, to remind people that concessions are available. Unless you can get other advertising donated, we don't recommend paying for your own advertising, because it is difficult to recover the added cost in extra sales.

When the concession stand is open, you'll want to **post clear signs everywhere people can see them**. Obviously, you'll need a large, clear sign near the stand so everyone can identify it. If your stand is not in clear sight from the seating and lanes, make sure to post signs giving directions with arrows pointing to the concession stand, making it easy to find, as well as reminding everyone that concessions are available. You can also incorporate advertisements into your direction signs, letting customers know what deals you are running, or what items are available. Pictures of hot dogs and popcorn make great visual aids for these posters, or you can attach empty candy wrappers as suggestions for purchases.

At the stand, you'll want a **nice large sign to identify the stand from a distance, as well as a large, easy to read sign naming the items and their prices**. Manufacturers spend millions of dollars researching, developing, branding and advertising their packaging, so you should take advantage of that free marketing by **prominently displaying sample products where they are easy to see**. Customers are more likely to purchase products with packaging they've seen on television, billboards or online if they can see them clearly displayed at your stand, instead of just listed on a sign and hidden in a box under the counter. Artistic arrangements of products will also help them to sell, especially if they are clearly in view of children, who are shorter than adults and can't always see as well.

10 ACCOUNTING

Because you're raising funds for a non-profit organization, you'll need to do some basic accounting, making sure you are actually making money, and that no one is stealing from you. Your organization's treasurer is a good resource to help you get started with the basics, but you don't have to be a CPA to get started.

Since you're dealing with cash, you'll have to keep track of how much you have, and insure no one is taking any of it. There are two simple numbers you'll want to keep track of, and a few other numbers that you can find with simple calculations. First, you need to **track how much money you start with in the cash drawer**. You'll need to start each day with some small bills and coins so you can make change, so someone needs to go to the bank and withdraw change, and put it in the cash drawer. Make sure you collect the receipts from the bank so you know how much cash you're starting with each day; if there is enough change at the end of each day to "seed" the next day, you need a written record of how much was left for the next day. Second, you need to know **how much money is left in the cash drawer at the end of the day**. We recommend providing the last shift of volunteers with a simple form to record the amount of cash in the drawer, as well as a place for at least 2 volunteers to sign that they've both counted the money and agree on the amount. The amount on that form should match the bank deposit slip (subtract the next day's change if you leave it in the drawer), so you know that no money disappears on the trip to the bank. For example, if you start with $30 in change, and have $150 at the end of the day, you should have a bank withdrawal receipt for $30 change, a bank deposit slip for $150, and a signed volunteer form for $150 of cash at the end of the shift (your actual sales for the day would be $150 - $30 = $120).

The other accounting area you'll have to deal with is product inventory.

One of your volunteers will receive a receipt when they purchase the food and supplies. In the simplest approach, all you have to do is **reimburse the person who is purchasing and delivering the products, keeping their receipt for your records.** When they deliver their purchases, a second person signs the receipt to verify that everything on the receipt was delivered (that is, nothing was stolen from the purchases). That signed receipt is then submitted to the organization's treasurer for reimbursement, so the person making the purchases can get their money back.

If you want to get more sophisticated, you can also take occasional inventories of the stock. When you take inventory, you count and write down how much is left of each product. Taking an inventory allows you to determine what is selling well, and how much profit you're making, but it is time consuming, both to count and to do the math, so you'll have to decide how often makes sense for your organization. You can do inventory counts as often as every shift change, or as little as once a season, depending on how much volunteer time you have available and your desire to know exactly what is selling in the stand.

That's all of the accounting you need to know to run a successful concession stand. The rest of this chapter is optional, advanced accounting, so we won't be hurt if you skip ahead to the next chapter (really!). Because you will start or end with extra food, your actual profit depends on your starting and ending inventory. For example, if you purchase $100 worth of food, and sell $100 worth of food, it seems like you didn't make any money, but you should have about $50 worth of food left over, which you can sell for another $100 later. On the other hand if you start with $100 of food from the last time, and sell all of it for $200, it looks like you had $200 of profit, but you have to account for the food you started with, and your true profit is actually $100.

In order to calculate your actual profit, you'll need the following information (which you've already collected):

- How much money you took in (called Income), which is the amount of money in the cash drawer at the end of the day, minus the change you started with.
- How much you spent on products and supplies (called Cost), which is on the receipt from the store (get a copy before it is submitted for reimbursement).
- The number of each product you started with (Starting Inventory)
- The number of each product left over (Ending Inventory)
- The cost of each product (usually listed on the store receipt)

To find your profit, you start with the Income. From the Income, you subtract the Cost, add the value of the starting inventory (number of each product times the cost for that product), and subtract the value of the ending inventory. Inventory values are the number of items times their cost, all added together, which is a little tricky, so if you need help determining the inventory values, check out the math chapter. The formula for Profit is: **Profit = Income − Cost + Starting Inventory − Ending Inventory**. Accountants like to show it like this:

Income
- Cost
+ Starting Inventory
- Ending Inventory

Profit

For example, if you have Income of $130 in the cash drawer, the Cost of your food was $60, your Starting Inventory was $10, and your Ending Inventory was $15, then your profit was $130 -$60 +$10 - $15 = $65.

To determine how much each volunteer is earning you per hour, divide the day's profit by the number of volunteer hours, or **Earnings per Hour = Profit / Number of hours**. In our example, if your volunteers worked four hours, they earned $65 / 4 hours = $16.25 per hour, which is much better than most car washes.

If you really want to get sophisticated, your percentage of profit (% profit) is the Profit divided by the Cost and adjusted Inventory, times 100, with the formula looking like this: **% Profit = (Profit / (Cost − Starting Inventory + Ending Inventory)) X 100**. In our example, the % Profit is ($65 / ($60 - $10 + $15)) X 100 = 100% profit, which means that for every dollar we spent on food, we made two dollars.

11 SIXTH GRADE MATH

Rick's father taught commercial photography, which involves math using fractions. Because everyone learns how to add and multiply fractions in sixth grade and then promptly forgets, he taught a class nicknamed "Sixth Grade Math." In his honor, we've added this section to review some of the math you'll need to run a concession stand, just in case it's been a while since sixth grade, or you don't have access to a motivated sixth grader.

How do I compare the price of different sizes (determining price per ounce)?

When you're deciding what to charge for your products, it is useful to compare prices with vending machines and other local concession stands - but the packages may not be the same sizes. By calculating the price per ounce, you can determine what to charge for the size you have. To determine the price per ounce, you divide the price by the number of ounces:

Price per ounce = Price ÷ Number of ounces
> Or

Price per ounce = Price / Number of ounces

For example, if the vending machine has a king sized 5 ounce candy bar for \$1.75, the price per ounce would be \$1.75 ÷ 5 ounces = \$0.35 per ounce. To find out how much to charge for your products, multiple the competitors' price per ounce times the number of ounces in your product:

Your Product Price = (Competitor's price per ounce) X (Number of ounces in your product)
> Or

Your Product Price = (Competitor's price per ounce) * (Number of ounces in your product)

In our example, if you have a normal sized 3 ounce candy bar, you should charge ($0.35 per ounce) X (3 ounces) = $1.05 per candy bar. By using these calculations, you can set your prices based on local competition, even if your product sizes are different from theirs.

How do I add extra costs to get the total cost of my product?

Some of your products will cost more to serve than just what you pay by the case. For example, you may have to add the cost of buns, disposable containers, utensils and condiments. In this section we'll look at how to add these costs into your cost per item, making sure you are charging enough to cover all of your costs. To determine the starting cost per item, divide the total price for the case by the number of items in a case:

Cost per item = Cost per case ÷ Number of items in the case

For example, if you buy a case of 30 candy bars for $16, the price per candy bar is $16 ÷ 30 = $0.53 per candy bar. Another good example is hot dogs. If you buy a package of 8 hot dogs for $2.50, the cost per hot dog is $2.50 ÷ 8 = $0.31 per hot dog. But you can't just sell a plain hot dog; you need to sell them with buns and wrappers, so you have to add in those costs. To determine the real cost for a product, divide the extra costs by the number of extra items, and add that to the cost of the product:

Real Cost = (Cost of accessories ÷ Number of accessories) + Starting cost per item

Using our hot dog example, if buns come in packs of 10 for $1, the real cost of a hot dog and bun is ($1 per pack of buns ÷ 10 Buns) + $0.31 per hot dog = $0.41 per hot dog and bun. If the product has more accessories, you just keep on adding the extra costs. If we add foil wrappers to our hotdogs, at $3 for 100 sheets, the hot dogs now cost ($3 per pack of foil ÷ 100 Sheets) + $0.41 per hot dog and bun = $0.44 per hot dog with bun and wrapper. You would use a similar calculation to add napkins and condiments (For liquids like ketchup and mustard, look at the number of servings printed on the bottle). You would use the same kind of calculations to add cups and cream to coffee, or salt, oil and bags to popcorn.

How Do I Find the Value of My Inventory?

If you really want to know how much you've earned at your concession stand, you need to adjust for the value of your starting and ending inventory. To value your inventory, you need the following information:
1. How many you have of each item
2. The cost of each item

The first is easy, but time consuming – for each product, you count how many you have, and write down that number. We've already talked about finding the cost of each item - divide the total price for the case by the number of items in a case, or:

Cost per item = Cost per case ÷ Number of items in the case

It helps to make a list of each product and how much they cost, then write down the number of each item when you do inventory:

Product	Cost per Item	Number of Items	Inventory Value of Products
Candy Bar	0.53	10	$5.30
Hot Dogs	0.44	20	$8.80
Sodas	0.57	30	$17.10

To find the value of a product, you multiply the Cost per Item times the Number of Items:

Value of Product = (Cost per Item) X (Number of Items)

To get the value of the entire inventory, just add up the value of all the separate products. For our example above, this would be $5.30 + $8.80 + $17.10 = $31.20.

If you're a "techie," you may even want to set up some of these calculations in a spreadsheet. We certainly recommend a spreadsheet as a timesaver if you're calculating the value of your inventory often. However, if you like to keep things simple, you should be just fine with paper, pencil, and a standard calculator.

12 CONCLUSION

Well, that should be everything you need to know to start and run a successful fundraising concession stand. If you're just starting out, keep things small and simple; it's OK if you sell everything out the first time, but much harder to recover if you have three times more food than you can sell. Over time, observe what sells well, and slowly experiment with different products and pricing ideas. Take good care of your volunteers, and listen to their ideas for improvement. Have fun, and raise plenty of cash for your organization.

APPENDIX A – WORKSHEET: SHOULD I START A CONCESSION STAND?

There are many costs associated with starting a concession stand, so it is good to understand all of your costs before starting out. Once you understand all of your costs, you can determine whether you can still make money, and if the amount you'll make is worth the time you and your volunteers invest. We've provided the following worksheet to help you gather costs and make that decision. If you need help estimating costs and sales, refer to the chapter on Stocking.

Startup Costs	
_____	What is my cost to rent or build a facility, or purchase tables and a canopy?
_____	What do I have to pay for cooking equipment (e.g. microwave)?
_____	What are my costs for other equipment (coolers, cart & utensils)?
_____	Cost of the season's first food purchase
_____	Cost of supplies for the season (cups, napkins, cleaning supplies, trash bags)
_____	Amount of change starting in the cash drawer the first day
_____	Total Startup Costs (add all of the above together)
Seasonal Costs	

_____	Cost of all remaining food for the season
_____	Fees, Deposits, and other non-food seasonal costs
_____	Utilities costs (electricity, trash removal)
_____	Total Seasonal Costs (add all of the seasonal costs together)
Total Costs	
_____	Total Startup Costs (from above)
_____	Total Seasonal Costs (from above)
_____	Total Costs (add the two lines above together)
Total Income	
_____	What income do I expect from selling products (typically about twice the food costs)?
_____	Cash drawer change, deposits returned, and other non-sales money received back at the end of the season
_____	Total Income (add the two lines above together)
Total Profit	
_____	Total income (from above)
_____	Total Costs (from above)
_____	Total Profit (subtract the total costs from the total income)

Once you've completed the worksheet, ask yourself these questions:

- Is my organization able to provide enough cash up front to cover the total startup costs?
- If the startup costs are high, is my organization willing to take a loss or break even the first season, as an investment in the concession stand?
- Is the total profit for the season worth the amount of time that volunteers will have to spend working on the concession stand?

APPENDIX B – LIST OF STARTUP ITEMS

There are a number of items you might need to start up your concession stand. Just in case you've forgotten something, here is a list of items you might want to consider adding to your shopping list:

- Cooking and Food Preparation Equipment
    - Commercial popcorn popper
    - Hot dog grill or roller
    - Crock pots
    - Microwave
    - Commercial Coffee Pot
    - Gas grill or camp stove and propane
    - Extension cords
    - Utensils for cooking (spoons, tongs, spatulas, etc)
    - Scissors or knife for opening packages
    - Can opener
    - Disposable gloves
- Display, Storage and Transportation
    - Tables or counter tops
    - Canopy, awning or portable building
    - Display cases or racks
    - Menu and price signs
    - Cart to transport heavy products (especially beverages)
    - Trailer or portable stand
    - Shelving
    - Coolers, beverage icing tubs or refrigerator/freezer
    - Napkin dispenser
    - Cup dispenser
    - Weights to hold down disposable plates in the wind.
- Administration and Finance

- o Cash Box or cash drawer
- o Calculator
- o Markers, pens and paper (including a permanent marker)
- o Tape to reseal boxes and hang signs
- Miscellaneous
  - o Trash cans
  - o Paper towels
  - o Dish soap and scrubbing utensils
  - o Napkins
  - o Disposable cups and containers
  - o Condiments
  - o Food

ABOUT THE AUTHORS

Rick Kraemer is an electrical engineer and entrepreneur with an MBA from Golden Gate University. He and his wife Becky are community leaders and volunteers in northern California. Together they have written multiple books on subjects like parenting, cancer caregiving, and the true nature of masculinity. Rick and Becky have been married since 1989, and are the parents of three teenage children, one girl and two boys, who they've raised from scratch. They enjoy water sports, many forms of exercise, animated conversations while walking by the lake, and volunteering in the community.

www.ingramcontent.com/pod-product-compliance
Lightning Source LLC
Chambersburg PA
CBHW051225170526
45166CB00005B/2051